# What The Hi story

# You are about to read the coolest History series ever written.

*"Make History Wavy again"*

# THE INCA EMPIRE

*The Rise and Fall of One of the World's Greatest Civilizations*

# Introduction

The Inca Empire was like, one of the most epic civilizations ever, right? It all started in the early 1400s when this dude named Pachacuti decided to expand his territory. He was like, "Let's make this place lit!" So, he and his crew built massive cities, like Cusco, which was the capital and totally the heart of the empire. They even created a super cool road system that stretched over 25,000 miles! That's like driving across the whole country, but way more intense.

But then, in the 1500s, things got real messy. Spanish conquistadors, led by Francisco Pizarro, rolled in and were like, "Surprise! We want your gold!" The Incas were totally unprepared for this invasion, and it was a total bummer. The empire fell apart faster than a bad TikTok trend, and just like that, one of the greatest civilizations in history was gone. What really happened to the Inca treasures? And how did they manage to build such an incredible society without modern tech? The answers are waiting to be uncovered, and trust, it's gonna be a wild ride!

# TABLE OF CONTENTS

# CHAPTER 1

*The Rise of the Inca Empire: How a
Small Tribe Became a Powerful
Civilization*

Once upon a time, in the heart of the
Andes Mountains, there was a small tribe
called the Incas. Imagine a group of people

living high up in the clouds, surrounded by majestic peaks and deep valleys. They were like tiny ants marching along the mountain paths, unaware of the greatness that awaited them. But little did they know, this small tribe would grow into one of the most powerful civilizations in the world!

The story of the Inca Empire begins in the early 15th century when a clever and ambitious leader named Pachacuti took charge. Picture him as a wise captain steering his ship through stormy seas, determined to find new lands. Under his guidance, the Incas began to expand their territory, conquering neighboring tribes and bringing them into their fold. It was as if Pachacuti had a magical map, guiding him to lands filled with resources and fertile soil.

The Incas were brilliant builders, creating roads that snaked through the mountains like ribbons of silver. These roads connected cities and allowed for the easy movement of people and goods. Imagine walking along these paths, feeling the cool mountain breeze on your face, as you pass colorful markets filled with fresh fruits and vibrant textiles. The

Incas traded everything from potatoes to gold, and their economy flourished like a blooming garden.

But the Incas were not just skilled traders; they were also masterful engineers. They built impressive structures, like the famous city of Machu Picchu, perched high above the clouds. Imagine standing in this ancient city, surrounded by stone walls and terraces, as the sun rises and casts a golden glow over the landscape. It's a breathtaking sight, a reminder of the incredible achievements of the Inca people.

One of the most fascinating things about the Incas was their connection to the land. They believed that the mountains were sacred and that their ancestors lived in the peaks. The Incas were like guardians of the Earth, respecting nature and understanding that their survival depended on it. They farmed the steep hillsides using a technique called terrace farming, creating flat areas where they could grow crops. Picture rows of corn and potatoes growing in perfect harmony with the mountain, a testament to their ingenuity and respect for the environment.

As the Inca Empire grew, it became a melting pot of cultures. Different tribes brought their customs and traditions, creating a rich tapestry of life. Imagine a vibrant festival where people danced, sang, and shared stories around a roaring fire. The Incas embraced diversity, and their empire became a place where everyone could contribute to the greater good.

However, with great power comes great responsibility. The Incas faced challenges from rival tribes and the harshness of nature.

They had to be brave, like warriors facing a fierce storm. But through teamwork and determination, they overcame obstacles and continued to thrive.

The rise of the Inca Empire teaches us an important lesson: even the smallest beginnings can lead to great things. Just like the Incas, we can achieve our dreams by working hard, respecting our environment, and embracing the diversity around us.

**Key Takeaway:** The Inca Empire reminds us that with determination and teamwork, we can grow from small beginnings into something great, just like the mighty mountains that surrounded them.

# CHAPTER 2

## *The Sacred City of Cusco: The Heart of the Inca Empire*

Imagine a city nestled high in the Andes Mountains, where the air is crisp and the sky is a brilliant blue. This is Cusco, the sacred heart of the Inca Empire, a place that once thrummed with life and power. Long ago, the Incas built this magnificent city, and it became the center of their world, like the beating heart in the chest of a giant.

As you walk through the cobblestone streets of Cusco, you can almost hear the whispers of the past. Picture the bustling markets filled with colorful textiles, where women in vibrant skirts traded fruits and vegetables, their laughter echoing in the air. Imagine the strong men, wearing ponchos, carrying heavy stones to build grand temples and palaces. Cusco was not just a city; it was a thriving hub of culture, trade, and spirituality.

The Incas believed that Cusco was the center of the universe, a sacred place where the earth and the sky met. The city was designed in the shape of a puma, an important animal in Inca mythology, symbolizing strength and power. The Sacsayhuamán fortress, perched on a hill overlooking the city, was like the puma's head, watching over its territory. With its massive stone walls, expertly crafted without any mortar, Sacsayhuamán was a marvel of engineering. Can you imagine how the Incas moved those enormous stones? They didn't have cranes or modern machines, just their strength, ingenuity, and teamwork!

As the sun set behind the mountains, Cusco transformed into a magical place. The golden light bathed the city, making the stones glow like treasure. In the heart of Cusco stood the Coricancha, the Temple of the Sun, adorned with gold and silver. The Incas worshipped Inti, the Sun God, believing he brought warmth and life to their crops. The temple was a dazzling sight, filled with shimmering offerings and the sounds of prayers rising to the heavens. Can you feel the excitement in the air as the Incas celebrated their connection to the sun?

But what made Cusco truly special was its people. The Incas were master builders, farmers, and astronomers. They created a vast network of roads and bridges that connected their empire, stretching across mountains and valleys like a spider's web. This allowed them to trade goods, share ideas, and communicate with one another. Imagine traveling along those ancient roads, surrounded by breathtaking views of mountains and rivers, meeting people from different cultures along the way. It was a world full of adventure!

Yet, the story of Cusco is also a reminder of the fragility of greatness. The Inca Empire faced challenges, including invasions and natural disasters. Just like a beautiful flower can be crushed by a strong wind, even the mightiest empires can fall. As we think about Cusco, we must ponder our own actions. How do we treat our homes, our communities, and our planet? Are we taking care of the treasures around us, just like the Incas cherished their sacred city?

Cusco stands today as a symbol of resilience and heritage. It invites us to explore its ancient streets and learn from its history. When we visit, we can honor the spirit of the Incas, remembering their incredible achievements and the lessons they left behind.

**Key Takeaway:** The story of Cusco teaches us that greatness can be built through teamwork, creativity, and respect for our surroundings. Just like the Incas, we should cherish and protect our homes and communities, ensuring that they thrive for future generations.

# CHAPTER 3

*Engineering Marvels: The Incredible*

*Inca Roads and Bridges*

Imagine standing at the foot of a towering mountain, the sun shining brightly above, casting a warm glow on the lush green valleys below. In the distance, you can see a narrow path winding its way up the steep slopes, disappearing into the clouds. This path is not just any ordinary trail; it is part of the incredible road system built by the ancient Inca Empire, a feat of engineering that still amazes people today!

The Incas were master builders, and their roads were like the veins of a giant living organism, connecting the heart of their empire to every corner of the land. Stretching over 25,000 miles, these roads were crafted with such precision that they could withstand the test of time and the forces of nature. Imagine walking along these paths, where every step tells a story of the past, and every stone has been placed with care and purpose.

One of the most impressive aspects of the Inca roads was how they adapted to the rugged terrain of the Andes Mountains. These roads climbed steep hills, crossed rushing rivers, and even navigated through dense forests. To do this, the Incas built incredible bridges that seemed to float in the air! Some were made of strong grasses and vines, woven together with such skill that they could hold the weight of people and animals crossing above roaring rivers. Picture yourself walking across one of these swaying bridges, the sound of the water crashing below you, as you marvel at the ingenuity of the Inca engineers.

But the Inca roads were more than just pathways; they were vital for communication and trade. The Incas used a system of messengers called "chasquis," who ran along these roads to deliver important messages and goods. Imagine a young chasqui, his heart racing as he dashes through the mountains, carrying a message from one village to another. His feet pound against the ancient stones, and he navigates the twists and turns of the road, just like a hero in a grand adventure!

The roads also connected the Inca people to their sacred sites, where they worshipped the sun and other deities. Along these paths, you could find small shrines and resting places, where travelers could stop to pray and reflect. The roads were not just functional; they were also spiritual, inviting everyone to be part of a larger story, one that stretched across mountains and valleys.

As we think about the incredible engineering of the Inca roads and bridges, we can't help but wonder about the people who built them. What motivated them to create such masterpieces? Perhaps it was their love for their land, their desire to connect with each other, or their need to share their culture and traditions. The Inca roads remind us that, just like the Incas, we too can build connections with others, no matter how challenging the journey may be.

Now, let's take a moment to reflect on the importance of these engineering marvels. The

Inca roads were not just a way to get from one place to another; they represented the unity and strength of a civilization. They showed how people can come together to create something extraordinary, even in the face of obstacles.

**Key Takeaway:** The Inca roads and bridges teach us that with teamwork, creativity, and determination, we can overcome challenges and build connections that last a lifetime.

# CHAPTER 4

## *Machu Picchu: The Lost City of the Incas and Its Mysteries*

High up in the misty mountains of Peru, where the clouds kiss the peaks and the sun paints the sky in hues of gold, lies a hidden treasure of the ancient world: Machu Picchu.

Imagine standing at the edge of a towering cliff, surrounded by lush green valleys and the whisper of the wind. This remarkable city, often called "The Lost City of the Incas," was built over 500 years ago and is still a wonder today.

Picture this: the Inca people, skilled builders and farmers, carefully crafted Machu Picchu from the stones of the mountains. They didn't have modern machines or tools like we do now. Instead, they used their hands, simple tools, and a lot of teamwork to create this breathtaking place. It was like building a giant puzzle, where each stone fit perfectly into the next, creating walls that have stood strong against time and nature.

But why did they choose such a high and remote location? Some say it was a sacred place, close to the heavens where the sun god, Inti, could watch over them. Others believe it was a secret hideout, a place where the Inca rulers could escape and keep their treasures safe from invaders. As you walk through the ancient pathways, you can almost hear the echoes of laughter and the bustling of life that once filled the air.

One of the most fascinating things about Machu Picchu is how it was rediscovered. In 1911, an adventurous American explorer named Hiram Bingham set out to find this lost city. Imagine him, trekking through thick jungles, climbing steep mountains, and facing the unknown! When he finally stumbled upon Machu Picchu, it was like finding a hidden gem sparkling in the rough. He was amazed by the beauty and mystery of the place, and his discovery brought the ancient Inca civilization back into the world's spotlight.

As you explore Machu Picchu, you might notice the clever ways the Incas adapted to their environment. They built terraces on the mountainsides to farm crops like potatoes and corn, which helped them survive in the thin mountain air. Each terrace was like a step in a giant staircase, allowing rainwater to flow down and nourish the plants. This ingenuity shows us how connected the Incas were to nature, and it reminds us of the importance of taking care of our planet.

Walking through the city, you'll find the Temple of the Sun, where the Incas worshipped their sun god. Imagine the priests, dressed in colorful robes, performing rituals and offering gifts to the sun. The temple is designed in a way that on the summer solstice, the sun shines through a special window, illuminating the altar. It's as if the sun itself was blessing the Incas and their way of life.

But Machu Picchu is not just a place of beauty; it is also shrouded in mysteries. Why did the Incas abandon this magnificent city? Some believe that the arrival of Spanish conquerors forced them to flee, while others think that diseases brought by outsiders may have played a role. The truth remains a puzzle, waiting for curious minds to uncover its secrets.

As you stand atop the mountain, gazing out over the sprawling landscape, you might wonder about your own place in the world. Why did the Incas build such a magnificent city? What dreams and stories did they hold in their hearts? Just like the Incas, we all have our own stories to tell and mysteries to explore.

Machu Picchu invites us to think about our connection to the past and the lessons we can learn from those who came before us. It reminds us that even in the face of challenges, creativity and teamwork can lead to extraordinary achievements.

**Key Takeaway:** Machu Picchu teaches us that great things can be built with teamwork and respect for nature. It also reminds us to explore our world and learn from the past, as every story holds a mystery waiting to be discovered.

# CHAPTER 5

## *The Inca Religion: Gods, Rituals, and Sacred Offerings*

In the heart of the Andes Mountains, where the peaks kissed the sky and the valleys sang with life, there thrived a civilization known as the Inca Empire. This empire was not just famous for its grand cities and impressive stone structures; it was also known for its rich and colorful tapestry of beliefs, rituals, and a deep connection to the divine. Welcome to the world of Inca religion, a fascinating journey into the hearts and minds of a people who looked to the heavens for guidance and inspiration.

Imagine waking up in a small village nestled among the clouds, where the sun rises like a golden orb, casting a warm glow on the earth. As the villagers stir from their slumber, they begin their day with a simple yet powerful act: a prayer. The Incas believed that their world was filled with gods and spirits that watched over them. There was Inti, the Sun God, who brought warmth and light to their crops, and Pachamama, the Earth Mother, who nourished the land and provided for their needs. Every sunrise was a reminder of their gratitude, a chance to honor these powerful beings.

The Incas were not just passive followers of their gods; they engaged in vibrant rituals that connected them to the divine. Picture a bustling plaza filled with people dressed in colorful garments, their faces painted with bright hues. They gathered for a festival, the air alive with the sounds of music and laughter. Drums thumped like the heartbeat of the earth, and flutes sang sweet melodies that floated into the sky. This was a time for celebration, a time to give thanks for the blessings of the gods.

But not all rituals were joyous. The Incas understood that life was a delicate balance, and sometimes, they believed that the gods needed to be appeased. In times of drought or disaster, they would perform elaborate ceremonies, which could include offerings of food, textiles, or even precious items like gold and silver. Imagine a priest standing at the top of a mountain, holding a beautifully woven cloth filled with gifts for the gods. With a heart full of hope, he would release the offerings into the wind, sending them soaring into the sky as a message of devotion.

One of the most dramatic moments in Inca religion was the ritual of human sacrifice. While this may sound shocking, the Incas believed that offering a life was the ultimate gift to their gods. The chosen individuals, often children or young adults, were treated with great honor in the days leading up to the sacrifice. They were given special foods and clothing, celebrated as heroes who would help maintain the balance of the universe. The ceremony itself was solemn and filled with deep meaning, a moment where the community came together to honor their beliefs and the power of the divine.

The Incas also had a special connection to the mountains, which they viewed as sacred. They believed that each peak held its own spirit, a guardian watching over the land and its people. This reverence for nature was woven into their daily lives. Farmers would often make small offerings to the mountains before planting their seeds, asking for a bountiful harvest. They understood that they were part of a larger web of life, where every action had consequences.

As the sun set behind the majestic Andes, painting the sky in shades of orange and purple, the Incas would gather for their evening prayers. They would light candles and offer incense, creating a fragrant cloud that spiraled upwards, carrying their hopes and dreams to the heavens. They believed that their words were heard, that their gods were listening, and that they were never alone in the vastness of the universe.

Inca religion was not just a set of beliefs; it was a way of life. It taught them to respect the earth, to honor their ancestors, and to seek harmony with the world around them. The rituals and offerings were a reflection of their love for the land and their desire to live in balance with nature. As we ponder the lessons of the Incas, we can ask ourselves: How do we honor the world we live in? What rituals or practices can we create to show our gratitude for the beauty around us?

**Key Takeaway:** The Inca religion teaches us the importance of gratitude, respect for nature, and the belief that we are all connected in a larger story. Just as the Incas honored their gods and the earth, we too can find ways to appreciate and protect our planet and the life it supports.

# CHAPTER 6

## *Agriculture in the Sky: Terracing and Farming Techniques of the Incas*

Imagine standing high up in the Andes Mountains, where the air is crisp and the clouds seem to brush against the jagged peaks. Below you, a breathtaking landscape unfolds—a patchwork of green and brown, like a giant quilt stitched together by nature's hand. This is the heart of the Inca Empire, where the Incas transformed steep, rocky mountainsides into fertile fields through an incredible technique called terracing.

Terracing is like creating giant steps on the side of a mountain. The Incas built these steps, or terraces, to hold the soil in place, preventing it from washing away during heavy rains. It was as if they were crafting a staircase to the sky, allowing them to climb higher and higher into the clouds while still growing food. Can you picture farmers walking up and down these terraces, tending to their crops, surrounded by the beauty of the mountains? They cultivated potatoes, corn, and quinoa, using the natural sunlight and the rich soil to nourish their families and their empire.

But how did the Incas manage to farm in such a challenging environment? They were like skilled artists, using their knowledge of the land to create a masterpiece of agriculture. The Incas understood that different crops needed different conditions to thrive. They planted their crops in rows, carefully choosing the right seeds for each terrace based on the amount of sunlight and moisture available. This thoughtful planning allowed them to grow a variety of foods, ensuring that their people were well-fed.

One of the most fascinating aspects of Inca agriculture was their ability to adapt to the changing seasons. They developed a system of irrigation, which is like giving water to the plants when they need it most. They built channels and canals that brought water from nearby rivers to their fields, creating a lifeline for their crops. Imagine the sound of water flowing through these channels, nourishing the earth and helping the plants grow tall and strong. It was a beautiful symphony of nature and human ingenuity.

As you explore the terraces, you might stumble upon a small village where the Incas lived. Picture a bustling community filled with laughter and hard work. The villagers would gather to celebrate the harvest, sharing stories and delicious meals made from the fruits of their labor. They understood the importance of working together, like a team of superheroes, each person playing a vital role in the success of their crops. Their unity was the key to thriving in such a demanding environment.

But there was more to Inca agriculture than just growing food. The Incas believed that the earth was a living being, and they treated it with great respect. They practiced a form of farming that was sustainable, meaning they took care of the land so it could take care of them. They rotated their crops, allowing the soil to rest and regain its nutrients, much like how we take breaks to recharge our energy. This harmony with nature ensured that their farming practices would last for generations.

As you gaze out over the terraces, you might wonder: how did the Incas know so much about their land? The answer lies in their deep connection to the earth and their keen observations of the world around them. They were like scientists, studying the stars, the weather, and the plants. They passed down their knowledge through stories and traditions, ensuring that each generation would carry on the wisdom of their ancestors.

In the end, the Incas taught us that farming is not just about planting seeds and waiting for them to grow. It's about understanding the land, working together, and respecting the delicate balance of nature. Their agricultural techniques were a testament to their ingenuity and creativity, showing us that even in the toughest environments, we can thrive if we work in harmony with the world around us.

**Key Takeaway:** The Incas transformed steep mountains into fertile fields through terracing and sustainable farming practices, teaching us the importance of teamwork, respect for nature, and the value of knowledge passed down through generations.

# CHAPTER 7

## *The Language of the Incas: Quechua and Its Cultural Significance*

Imagine standing high in the Andes Mountains, where the air is crisp and the peaks seem to touch the sky. Below you, a vibrant world unfolds, filled with lush valleys and ancient stone cities. In this breathtaking landscape lived the Incas, a civilization that thrived long ago, and their voices echoed through the mountains in a beautiful language called Quechua.

Quechua is more than just a way to talk; it's a treasure chest of history and culture. When the Incas spoke Quechua, they shared stories of their gods, their daily lives, and their connection to the earth. It was like a magical thread that wove together their community, connecting people from different regions of their vast empire, which stretched from modern-day Peru to Ecuador and Bolivia.

Think of Quechua as a musical instrument, each word a note that creates a harmonious melody. When you say "sumaq," you're not just saying "beautiful"; you're capturing the essence of the vibrant flowers that bloom in the Andes. And when you say "Inti," you're calling upon the sun god, who was so important to the Incas that they celebrated him with grand festivals.

But how did the Incas use this language? Picture a bustling marketplace filled with colorful textiles, fragrant foods, and lively chatter. Quechua was the language of trade, where merchants would shout their prices and buyers would haggle with smiles and laughter. It was also the language of the farmers, who would sing songs to their crops, asking for rain and sunshine. Through these songs, they honored Pachamama, the earth goddess, showing their deep respect for nature.

The Incas didn't have a written language like we do today, but they used a clever system called quipus. These were colorful strings with knots tied in them, and they recorded information like numbers and important events. Imagine a giant abacus made of strings! Each knot and color told a story, allowing the Incas to keep track of everything from their harvests to their warriors. Even without written words, their culture thrived, thanks to the power of Quechua and the creativity of quipus.

As the Spanish conquistadors arrived in the 16th century, they brought their own language, Spanish, which began to overshadow Quechua. But the spirit of Quechua remained strong, like a river flowing through the mountains. Today, Quechua is still spoken by millions of people in the Andes, and it has become a symbol of pride and identity for many Indigenous communities. It reminds us that language is not just a tool for communication; it is a bridge to our ancestors and a pathway to understanding our place in the world.

Now, let's ponder a moment. Why is it important to preserve languages like Quechua? When a language fades away, it's like losing a piece of a puzzle that helps us understand the world. Each language carries its own unique way of seeing life, just like how different colors paint a beautiful picture. By learning and celebrating languages like Quechua, we honor the rich tapestry of human experience and ensure that future generations can hear the whispers of the past.

As we explore the significance of Quechua, we realize that language is a living, breathing part of who we are. It shapes our thoughts, our dreams, and our connections with one another. Just like the Incas, we too can use our words to build bridges and share our stories with the world.

**Key Takeaway:** The language we speak shapes our identity and connects us to our culture. Preserving languages like Quechua helps us honor the past and enrich our understanding of the world today.

# CHAPTER 8

## The Role of Women: Powerful Figures in Inca Society

In the heart of the majestic Andes Mountains, where the clouds seemed to kiss the peaks and the sun painted the sky in brilliant hues of orange and pink, there lived a remarkable civilization known as the Inca Empire. This empire, stretching across what is now Peru, was famous for its incredible achievements in architecture, agriculture, and engineering. But what many people might not know is that the Inca women played a vital role in this thriving society, wielding power and influence in ways that would surprise anyone who thought women were simply caretakers.

Imagine walking through a bustling Inca village. You can hear the laughter of children playing, the sizzling sounds of food being cooked, and the rhythmic sounds of weaving looms. As you stroll along the cobblestone streets, you might catch a glimpse of women wearing beautifully woven garments, their hands busy crafting intricate textiles that told stories of their culture. These women were not just skilled artisans; they were the backbone of their communities.

Inca society was structured like a giant tapestry, with each thread representing a different role. Women held significant positions within this tapestry, often managing households and making important decisions. They were responsible for weaving, cooking, and caring for the children, but they also played crucial roles in agriculture. Women helped plant and harvest crops, ensuring that their families had enough food to eat. They were like the roots of a sturdy tree, grounding their families and communities in times of need.

One of the most powerful women in Inca society was the "Coya," the queen. The Coya was not just the wife of the Sapa Inca, the emperor; she was a ruler in her own right. She had the authority to make decisions, manage land, and even lead armies if necessary. The Coya was a symbol of strength and wisdom, guiding her people with grace and courage. Imagine her standing tall, adorned in golden jewelry that sparkled like the stars, as she addressed her people with a voice that echoed through the valleys.

But the power of women didn't stop there. Inca women were also priests, serving in temples dedicated to the sun god, Inti. They participated in sacred rituals, ensuring that the gods were pleased and that the empire flourished. These women were like bright flames, illuminating the spiritual path for their people. Their devotion and commitment to their beliefs made them respected figures in society, and they often held significant sway over important matters.

The Inca Empire was a place where women could inherit property and pass it down to their daughters. This was quite different from many other cultures at the time. Imagine a young girl named Kusi, who inherited her mother's beautiful textiles and fields of corn. She would grow up knowing that she had the power to shape her own future, to create her own legacy. Kusi's story is just one of many that highlight the strength and resilience of Inca women.

However, it's essential to remember that life in the Inca Empire was not always easy. Women faced challenges, especially during times of war or famine. Yet, they showed incredible strength and determination, coming together to support one another. Picture a group of women gathered in a circle, sharing stories and laughter as they worked together to mend clothes or prepare food for their families. Their bond was like a woven blanket, providing warmth and comfort in difficult times.

As we explore the incredible roles that women played in the Inca Empire, we can't help but wonder about our own lives. How do we view the contributions of women in our world today? Are we celebrating their achievements and recognizing their importance? The story of the Inca women teaches us that everyone has a role to play in shaping society, and that power comes in many forms.

In the end, the legacy of Inca women is a testament to their strength, resilience, and unwavering spirit. They were powerful figures who contributed to the empire's success and inspired future generations to stand tall and embrace their potential. As we look up at the stars, we can remember that just like the women of the Inca Empire, we all have the power to shine brightly in our own lives.

**Key Takeaway:** Women in the Inca Empire were powerful figures who played essential roles in society, showing us that everyone has the ability to make a difference and contribute to their community.

# CHAPTER 9

## *The Fall of the Inca Empire: Conquest and Change*

In the heart of the Andes Mountains, where the air is crisp and the skies are painted with brilliant shades of blue, there once thrived a magnificent civilization known as the Inca Empire. Picture this: towering stone temples, lush green terraces filled with golden corn, and vibrant markets bustling with people. The Incas were masters of their land, creating a society rich in culture, art, and innovation. But as with many great stories, the tale of the Inca Empire took a dramatic turn, leading to its fall.

It was the early 1500s, a time when the world was filled with explorers seeking new lands and treasures. Among them was a man named Francisco Pizarro, a Spanish conquistador with a fierce ambition. He had heard whispers of a land filled with gold and riches, a place where the Incas worshipped the sun and built cities that seemed to touch the heavens. With a small group of soldiers, Pizarro set sail across the ocean, driven by dreams of glory.

Imagine the scene: Pizarro and his men arrived on the shores of Peru, their hearts pounding with excitement and fear. They were outnumbered, facing an entire empire, yet they carried weapons made of steel and horses that thundered like storm clouds. The

Incas, led by their mighty ruler Atahualpa, were initially curious about these strange newcomers. They welcomed Pizarro with open arms, believing he was a messenger from the gods. Little did they know, this encounter would change everything.

As Pizarro and Atahualpa met, a tense drama unfolded. Atahualpa, with his golden crown and regal presence, offered gifts of gold to the Spaniards, hoping to secure peace. But Pizarro, driven by greed, had other plans. He captured Atahualpa, holding him hostage in exchange for treasure. The Inca people, who once felt safe under their ruler's protection, were now filled with fear and confusion. How could their powerful leader be taken captive by these strange men?

In the days that followed, the Incas tried to rally together to rescue their king, but the Spanish soldiers were relentless. Pizarro's men attacked, using their advanced weapons and tactics. The Incas, though brave, were not prepared for this kind of warfare. The once-thriving empire began to crumble under the weight of betrayal and violence. It was as if a storm had swept through their land, leaving destruction in its wake.

But the fall of the Inca Empire was not just about battles and weapons. It was also a time of profound change. The arrival of the Spaniards brought new ideas, customs, and even diseases that the Incas had never encountered. Imagine a world where the familiar is suddenly replaced by the unknown. The Incas, who had thrived for centuries, now faced a new reality. Their rich traditions, their connection to the land, and their way of life were all at risk.

As the empire fell, the Incas showed incredible resilience. They adapted to the changes around them, blending their ancient beliefs with new influences. They learned to navigate this new world, finding ways to preserve their culture even in the face of adversity. It was a testament to the strength of the human spirit—how, even in the darkest of times, hope and determination can shine through.

The story of the Inca Empire teaches us important lessons about courage, change, and the consequences of our actions. It reminds us that history is not just a series of events but a tapestry woven with the lives and dreams of people. As we reflect on this chapter, we are invited to think about our own place in the world. How do we treat others? How do we learn from the past to create a better future?

**Key Takeaway:** The fall of the Inca Empire shows us that change can be both challenging and transformative. It teaches us the importance of understanding and respecting different cultures while reminding us that history shapes who we are today.

# CHAPTER 10

## *Legacy of the Incas: How Their Innovations Shape Our World Today*

Once upon a time, high in the Andes Mountains, there flourished a civilization known as the Incas. This remarkable empire was not just about grand temples and powerful rulers; it was also a place of incredible ideas and inventions that still touch our lives today. Imagine a world where every mountain path is a road to adventure, where farming is an art, and where communities work together like a perfectly tuned orchestra. The Incas created a legacy that resonates through time, and their innovations continue to shape our world in ways we might not even realize.

Picture yourself standing on a hillside, overlooking the breathtaking landscapes of Peru. The sun casts a golden hue over the terraced fields, where the Incas mastered the art of agriculture. They carved steps into the mountains, creating terraces that held water and soil, allowing crops to flourish in a place where the land was steep and rocky. This ingenious method not only provided food for their people but also prevented soil erosion. Today, farmers around the world still use similar techniques to grow crops on difficult terrains. Isn't it amazing how a simple idea from so long ago can still help feed people today?

Now, let's take a moment to explore the Inca roads, which were like the highways of their time. Imagine a network of paths stretching across the mountains, connecting cities and villages. These roads were built with such precision that they could withstand earthquakes, a common occurrence in the Andes. The Incas used stones that fit together perfectly, much like a puzzle, creating a solid foundation for their empire. This innovation allowed them to transport goods, messages, and even armies across vast distances. Today, we have roads and highways that connect our cities, but the Incas were pioneers in creating a system that brought their people together.

What would it be like if we had no roads? How would we visit friends or travel to new places?

As we journey deeper into the legacy of the Incas, we discover their incredible skills in architecture. The buildings they constructed, like the famous Machu Picchu, are marvels of engineering. These stone structures have stood the test of time, enduring centuries of weather and natural disasters. The Incas used a technique called "ashlar," where stones were cut to fit together without the use of mortar. This not only made their buildings strong but also gave them a unique beauty. Today, architects around the world study Inca techniques to inspire modern construction. Imagine living in a house that could withstand storms and earthquakes, just like the ancient Inca structures!

But the legacy of the Incas goes beyond agriculture, roads, and architecture. They also had a deep understanding of the stars and the seasons. The Incas were skilled astronomers, able to predict when to plant and harvest crops by observing the night sky. They built observatories and used the sun's position to create calendars. This connection to nature reminds us of the importance of understanding our environment. How often do we look up at the stars and wonder what secrets they hold? The Incas taught us that the universe is a vast playground of knowledge waiting to be explored.

In addition to their practical innovations, the Incas also emphasized community and cooperation. They believed that everyone had a role to play in their society, much like the parts of a beautiful symphony. This spirit of working together is something we can learn from today. How can we support each other in our own communities? The Incas showed us that by helping one another, we can create a stronger and more vibrant world.

As we reflect on the legacy of the Incas, we can't help but feel a sense of wonder about our place in the universe. Their innovations remind us that even the smallest ideas can have a big impact. Why do we continue to build upon the foundations laid by those who came before us? What will our own contributions be to the world? The story of the Incas is a reminder that we are all part of a larger tapestry, woven together by our shared history and aspirations.

**Key Takeaway:** The Incas taught us the importance of innovation, community, and respect for nature. By learning from their legacy, we can create a better future for ourselves and our planet.

# DEAR COOL KIDS/PARENTS

Thank you for choosing "What the History"! We hope this book has ignited a spark of wonder and motivation within you.

If you found this book captivating and believe in the transformative power of its message, we kindly ask for your support. Please consider leaving a glowing review on the platform where you purchased the book. Your review will help spread this message of empowerment to even more young readers, inspiring them to dream big and reach for the stars.

The core essence of this book - to inspire and uplift young minds - is what truly matters. We acknowledge that perfection is elusive, and we appreciate your understanding and forgiveness for any minor imperfections.

Thank you for being a part of our mission to nurture the brilliance and potential within the next generation. Your feedback will go a long way in helping us continue to provide captivating and transformative stories for young readers.

Made in the USA
Las Vegas, NV
07 January 2025

16013779R00056